KURUKSHETRA OF INVESTING

STRATEGY. PSYCHOLOGY. DECISIONS

Vishal Muralidharan

notionpress.com

INDIA • SINGAPORE • MALAYSIA

ISBN

Paperback 979-8-90431-093-6
Hardcase 979-8-90431-094-3

Contents

To my parents,

who built the foundation of values, resilience, and integrity on which everything in my life stands.

To my wife,

whose unwavering support and quiet strength sustained me through this journey.

To my clients,

whose trust over the years has been both a responsibility and a privilege, teaching me lessons no textbook ever could.

To the great investors, teachers, and thinkers who expanded my perspective and sharpened my judgement.

And with deepest gratitude to Maharshi Vyasa,

the eternal storyteller of the Mahabharata, whose timeless wisdom on human behaviour, choice, consequence, and dharma continues to guide us even today.

Foreword

Over the past three decades in the financial planning profession, I have had the privilege of working with thousands of families across different economic cycles, market conditions, and life situations. During this time, one truth has remained constant.

Financial success is rarely determined by how much a person earns or how much information they possess. It is shaped far more by behaviour. Patience during uncertainty, discipline during stability, and clarity during emotional moments often matter more than any product or strategy.

As a practitioner, I have seen intelligent individuals make avoidable mistakes and ordinary investors achieve extraordinary results simply by staying consistent. Markets change, regulations evolve, and new opportunities emerge, but human reactions to money remain remarkably similar across generations.

When my son joined this profession and began working alongside me, I observed the same patterns emerging through a new generation of investor interactions. His experiences reinforced what years of practice had already demonstrated: most financial struggles are not caused by lack of knowledge, but by internal conflict. Fear, comparison, pride, hesitation, and impatience continue to shape decisions at critical moments.

What makes this book distinctive is the framework it uses to explore that conflict. By drawing parallels between investing behaviour and the timeless narratives of the Mahabharata, it presents familiar financial challenges in a way that is both insightful and relatable. The epic is not treated as mythology or moral instruction, but as a profound study of human decision-making under pressure.

Over the years, I have come to believe that the role of a financial planner extends beyond recommending investments. It involves helping individuals remain steady when circumstances tempt them to act impulsively, and guiding them to stay aligned with long-term goals even when short-term emotions are intense. This book reflects that philosophy.

Readers will not find market predictions, product promotions, or promises of quick wealth. Instead, they will encounter lessons about discipline, clarity, adaptability, and self-awareness qualities that quietly determine financial outcomes over time. The stories presented here serve as mirrors, allowing investors to recognise patterns in their own behaviour before those patterns become costly.

I am proud to see these insights articulated in a form that can reach far beyond individual conversations. If this book encourages even a few readers to make calmer, more thoughtful financial decisions, it will have fulfilled a meaningful purpose.

Wealth creation is not a sprint driven by excitement, nor a gamble guided by hope. It is a long journey that rewards patience, prudence, and emotional balance. Books that help cultivate these qualities are rare and valuable.

I hope this work provides that guidance to all who read it.

Mr. Ganesan Muralidharan

Founder, GSM Investment Services

Financial Planning Professional with over three decades of experience

ACKNOWLEDGEMENTS

No meaningful work is created in isolation. This book is the result of influences, guidance, experiences, and support from many visible and invisible contributors who shaped both the ideas within these pages and the person who wrote them.

My deepest gratitude goes to my parents. To my father, whose integrity, discipline, and lifelong commitment to serving investors laid the foundation for my understanding of money beyond numbers. To my mother, whose quiet strength, patience, and unwavering support created the emotional stability that made long-term thinking possible. Whatever clarity exists in this book has roots in the values I learned at home.

To my wife, thank you for your love, patience, and understanding of the responsibilities and demands of my profession. Your steady support and trust give me the peace of mind needed to think, work, and grow. This book stands on that quiet foundation.

To my clients, past and present, this book owes you more than can be expressed. Every question, every concern, every moment of fear during market falls, and every expression of relief during recovery revealed the real challenges investors face. You showed me that financial decisions are rarely about products alone. They are about emotions, responsibilities, hopes, and uncertainties.

The patterns described in this book were learned from real lives, not theoretical models.

I am grateful to the many teachers, mentors, authors, and investment thinkers whose work has shaped modern understanding of markets and behaviour. Their ideas helped refine my thinking and prevented this book from becoming simplistic or one-dimensional.

Above all, I offer profound gratitude to Maharishi Vyasa, the author of the Mahabharata. The epic is not merely a story of war or heroism. It is an unparalleled study of human nature under pressure. Its characters reflect timeless patterns of thought, emotion, duty, ego, and consequence. Without that extraordinary work, this book would not exist. The lessons drawn here are only possible because of the depth and universality of the original narrative.

Finally, I thank you, the reader. By choosing to spend your time with these pages, you have entered a conversation that goes beyond investing. It is a conversation about judgement, discipline, and self-awareness. If this book helps you see your financial decisions more clearly, avoid unnecessary mistakes, or act with greater confidence and calm, then the effort behind it has been worthwhile.

No book can eliminate uncertainty. But the right perspective can make uncertainty manageable.

Thank you for being part of this journey.

Disclaimer (please Read Before Proceeding)

While reading this book, you may notice that some Concepts appear more than once. This is intentional.

The same concept is told using different stories on purpose. One story may not connect with you, but another one might.

Hearing the same idea through different stories helps it stay with you.

This book is written using Mahabharata stories along with my experience in observing investor behaviour.

It is not meant to be a religious or academic retelling of the epic.

If you are not familiar with the story mentioned in a chapter title, you may find it helpful to first take a quick look at that story online and then return to the chapter. This small step can make the lesson easier to follow and more meaningful.

If any story detail, sequence, or reference is incorrect, I sincerely apologise.

Any such mistake is unintentional.

I genuinely welcome your feedback.

If you notice anything that needs correction, please share it with us at.

gsminvestmentservices.01@gmail.com

I will research it carefully and correct it in future editions.

This book is written with respect, honesty, and a willingness to learn.

Thank you for reading it with an open mind.

PROLOGUE

The Kurukshetra war did not start suddenly. No one woke up one morning and decided to destroy an entire generation. The war was the result of many small decisions, hurt feelings, jealousy, pride, and injustice that kept building over time.

In the great kingdom of Hastinapura, there were two groups of princes from the same family. The Pandavas and the Kauravas. They grew up together, trained together, and were supposed to rule together. But things did not turn out that way.

The Pandavas were known for their courage, honesty, and unity. People respected them. This made Duryodhana, the eldest Kaurava, deeply insecure. He began to see them not as cousins, but as rivals who could take away his power.

After many conflicts, the kingdom was divided. The Pandavas were given a barren piece of land. Instead of complaining, they worked hard and built a beautiful and prosperous city called Indraprastha. Their success brought them fame and admiration across the land.

But it also made Duryodhana even more jealous.

Unable to defeat them openly, he planned something else. With the help of his uncle Shakuni, he invited Yudhishthira, the eldest Pandava, to a game of dice.

In those days, refusing such an invitation was seen as dishonourable.

The game was unfair from the beginning. Shakuni controlled the dice. Yet Yudhishthira continued to play, believing he must follow the rules of the game.

He lost everything.

First his wealth. Then his kingdom. Then his brothers. Then himself.

Finally, even Draupadi, their queen.

What followed was deeply humiliating and painful. Draupadi was insulted in front of the entire royal court while many elders remained silent. Though disaster was narrowly avoided, the Pandavas were punished with exile. They were sent away for thirteen years, with one final year to be spent in disguise.

The Pandavas endured all of it. They lived in forests. They suffered hardship. They completed the exile exactly as required. When they returned, they did not demand revenge or the entire kingdom. They asked only for what was rightfully theirs. Some traditions even say they were willing to settle for just five small villages.

Duryodhana refused.

Not because he needed the land. Not because compromise was impossible. But because giving even a small concession felt like losing face. His pride mattered more than peace.

One last attempt was made to avoid war. Krishna himself went to the Kaurava court as a messenger of peace. He did not threaten them. He did not demand surrender. He simply asked for a fair settlement so that countless lives could be saved.

Duryodhana rejected even this.

He would not give the Pandavas land equal to the tip of a needle.

At that moment, war became unavoidable.

Armies were gathered from across the land. Families split apart. Teachers faced their own students. Friends stood on opposite sides. The battlefield of Kurukshetra became the stage where years of unresolved conflict would finally explode.

By the time the war began, the real battle had already been fought in the minds of people. Kurukshetra was not just a fight for land. It was the result of ego, silence in the face of injustice, rigid promises, manipulation, hurt pride, and the inability to step back when it still mattered.

And this is why the Mahabharata still feels relevant today.

Because Kurukshetra is not only a place in history. It is a pattern that repeats in human life.

About The Author

Vishal Muralidharan is a second-generation financial planner at GSM Investment Services, a firm founded by his father, Mr. Ganesan Muralidharan, who has spent three decades building trust-based relationships in the financial planning profession.

Continuing this legacy, Vishal is a Certified Financial Planner (CFP®) and a Qualified Personal Finance Professional (QPFP®). He works closely with investors across diverse life stages, income levels, and market environments, helping them navigate long-term financial decisions with clarity and discipline.

From working closely with investors across different situations, one conclusion has become clear: financial success is rarely determined by intelligence, access to information, or the choice of products alone. It is largely shaped by behaviour.

Prior to this book, the author wrote two practical works on personal finance.

Retire Early Through Mutual Funds focuses on long-term wealth creation through disciplined investing, demonstrating how consistency and structured planning can support financial independence without speculation.

Goal Based Financial Case Studies presents real-life financial scenarios and illustrates how major goals such as retirement, education, and significant life expenses can be planned systematically. The book bridges the gap between theory and practical implementation.

While those works emphasise planning, structure, and execution, this book examines a deeper dimension. It does not focus on returns, performance comparisons, or numerical projections.

Instead, it explores behavioural finance: how people think, react, delay, panic, compare, or act emotionally when money is involved, and how these patterns influence long-term outcomes.

The author has a longstanding interest in the Mahabharata and its portrayal of human decision-making under pressure. He views the epic not merely as mythology, but as a timeless exploration of character, judgement, duty, ego, and consequence.

By connecting these insights with modern investing behaviour, this book seeks to help readers understand themselves before attempting to optimise returns. It is written for individuals who already know what they should do financially, but struggle to do it consistently.

Because when behaviour becomes disciplined and clear, financial outcomes tend to follow.

PREFACE

The War You Don't Realise You're Fighting

Kurukshetra is not just a place from history. It is a pattern that repeats in human life. Anyone who has tried to build wealth has fought this war at some point, not with weapons, but with fear, ego, impatience, comparison, temptation, and self-doubt. When you remove the armour, chariots, and battle formations from the Mahabharata, what remains feels surprisingly familiar. It looks very much like the way people behave with money.

I did not realise this at first. Over time, as I interacted with more investors, I began noticing the same patterns repeating again and again. Fear during market falls, overconfidence during rallies, confusion during uncertainty, tip-chasing, and reluctance to admit mistakes. My first reaction was simple. "They know better. Why are they doing thisṢ" Eventually, the answer became clear.

People don't make financial mistakes because they lack knowledge. They make mistakes because they are fighting an inner battle they don't recognise. Some investors are like Arjuna. They have skill and information, yet hesitate at the most critical moment. Some are like Yudhishthira. They become overconfident, believing they cannot lose, just before everything slips away. Some are like Karna. They cling to pride or rigid principles even when the cost becomes painfully obvious. Some are like Bhishma. They remain loyal to old decisions long after logic demands change. And some are like Duryodhana, so consumed by comparison that they lose peace, clarity, and judgment.

The investment world is not gentle. It tests ego, punishes hesitation, exposes overconfidence, makes delay expensive, and rewards discipline and clarity, often quietly. This book was born from one uncomfortable realisation. Wealth is not built only in spreadsheets or charts. It is built in the mind.

That is why I turned to the Mahabharata, not as mythology or religion, but as a study of human behaviour under pressure. It shows how intelligent people make poor decisions, how emotions overpower logic, and how clarity can change outcomes even in chaos.

Each chapter in this book tells a story from Kurukshetra and connects it to a real investing situation. These stories are not about heroes or villains. They are reflections. You will see parts of yourself in Arjuna's hesitation, Karna's pride, Bhishma's rigidity, and even Ashwatthama's rage. When you see it clearly, your own investing struggles begin to make sense.

If this book achieves only one thing, let it be this: investing is not a battle against the market. It is a battle within yourself. And just like in the Mahabharata, victory does not go to the strongest or the smartest. It goes to the one who understands the battlefield.

This is the Kurukshetra of investing. You entered it the moment you opened this book. Let us walk into it with clarity, not emotion.

HOW TO USE THIS BOOK

This is not a book to rush through. It is not a story you finish in one sitting.

And it is not a book full of quick tips.

Each chapter describes a situation you will face at some point in your investing journey.
So take it slowly.

Read One Chapter at a Time

Each chapter is complete on its own.

You don't have to remember everything at once.
Read one chapter.
Pause for a moment.

Ask yourself:
"Have I ever behaved like thisṢ"

The real value of this book is not finishing it fast.
It is understanding yourself honestly.

Don't Look for Tips. Look for Behaviour

This book will not tell you:

- what stock to buy
- which fund is best
- when the market will go up

Instead, it shows how people behave when money is involved:

- when fear takes over
- when ego interferes
- when impatience causes mistakes
- when delay becomes costly

Once you see these patterns, better decisions become easier.

Treat It Like a Mirror

These stories are not about judging anyone.

They show how normal people react under pressure.

- Sometimes you may see yourself in Arjuna.
- Sometimes in Karna.
- Sometimes in Bhishma or Ashwatthama.

That is completely normal.

- The goal is not to feel guilty.
- The goal is to become aware.
- And awareness is the first step toward better discipline.

Let It Slowly Change Your Behaviour

You don't have to apply everything immediately. Over time, let the lessons influence how you:

- react to news and noise
- handle losses
- deal with sudden opportunities
- evaluate advice
- stay committed to long-term goals

The aim is not perfection.

The aim is steady improvement.

If You Work With an Advisor, Discuss It

If you have a financial planner or advisor, talk about these ideas with them.

Not to analyse the stories.
But to ensure both of you think clearly during difficult situations.

Good investing is not only about products.
It is about making calm decisions together when pressure rises.

Final Thought

This book will not remove uncertainty. Nothing can do that.

But it can help you face uncertainty with:

- calm instead of panic
- patience instead of impulse
- judgment instead of rigid reactions

Life will bring many Kurukshetra moments again and again in different forms.
When they come, use this book not to fight harder, but to think more clearly.

That is how this book is meant to help you.

INTRODUCTION

Every generation thinks its problems are new. Every investor feels their fear, confusion, and mistakes are unique. But in reality, people have been struggling with the same inner battles for thousands of years. Only the situation has changed.

The Mahabharata may look like a story about war, kings, and warriors. But if you look closely, it is really about human behaviour. It shows how people act under pressure, how emotions affect decisions, how ego creates problems, and how patience or impatience can change outcomes.

This book does not retell the Mahabharata. It uses its stories to explain how people think and behave when money, uncertainty, and long-term decisions are involved.

Inside, you will find 25 simple stories, each connected to one practical lesson about building wealth and avoiding costly mistakes. No complex formulas. No predictions. Just clear insights about behaviour.

Because wealth is not built by intelligence alone. It is built by clear thinking and consistent actions.

This is not a book about war. It is about the battles you face every time you save, invest, worry, compare, or decide.

Understand those battles, and wealth stops feeling like luck. It starts feeling like clarity.

Turn the page. The journey begins.

Chapter 1

Bhishma's Vow: Flexibility matters more than rigid promises

Bhishma was one of the most respected people of his time. He was not greedy or power-hungry. People admired him for his honesty, discipline, and sense of duty.

When he was young, Bhishma made a huge promise to make his father happy. He said he would never become king and would never marry. This sacrifice made him famous. Everyone trusted him. People saw him as a man who would never go back on his word.

For many years, this promise worked well. But life did not stay the same.

Kings changed. Situations changed. Conflicts grew. Ego and politics increased. Wrong things started happening in the kingdom.

Bhishma saw all of it. He knew things were going in the wrong direction. He had the respect and authority to stop it.

But he didn't act.

Not because he supported the wrong actions. Not because he lacked courage. But because he felt trapped by the promise he had made long ago.

If he had stepped in strongly after King Pandu's death, or controlled Duryodhana early, the disaster that followed might have been avoided. The massive war that destroyed families and generations might never have happened.

By the time the war finally began, Bhishma was in a painful position.

He knew what was right.

He had the power to change things.

But he could not act differently because of a decision made decades earlier.

Bhishma did not fail because he was weak. He failed because he could not adjust.

His greatest strength, his promise, slowly turned into his biggest limitation.

THE INVESTMENT TRUTH: A Wrong Commitment Can Trap You for Years

Many investors unknowingly become Bhishma.

They make a decision at one point in life. A product. A strategy. A belief.

For example, a person may start a long-term policy believing it will secure the future. After a few years, he realises the returns are very low and no longer suit his goals. Yet he continues, not because it is beneficial, but because surrendering would mean accepting a loss and admitting the decision may not have been ideal.

Another person may buy a stock during a wave of positive news, expecting strong growth. Years later, the stock remains stagnant or even negative. Still, he refuses to sell. Not because the prospects are excellent, but because selling at a loss feels like defeat.

At that moment, both decisions may have been reasonable.

But over time, things change.

- Goals change.
- Income changes.
- Risk capacity changes.
- Markets change.
- Personal responsibilities change.

Yet the investor refuses to adapt. They say:

- "I have already committed."
- "I don't want to accept I was wrong."
- "I'll continue because I started this."
- "This is what I promised myself."

This is not discipline. This is rigidity.

Discipline follows logic. Rigidity follows ego. Many investors stay stuck in unsuitable investments not because they are profitable, but because exiting would hurt their self-image. Just like Bhishma, they know something is wrong. But they don't act. Because acting would mean breaking an old vow.

THE LESSON: Discipline Needs Flexibility to Survive

Bhishma teaches a difficult but necessary lesson. Commitment is powerful. But blind commitment is dangerous.

In investing:

- staying invested is discipline
- refusing to review is rigidity

- following a plan is strength
- refusing to update a plan is weakness

A good investor is not one who never changes. A good investor is one who changes **for the right reasons.** Markets reward adaptability, not stubbornness. Long-term success does not come from holding on at all costs. It comes from holding on **with awareness.** Bhishma's tragedy was not his vow. It was his refusal to revisit it.

This is your 1st lesson of Kurukshetra of investing:

Discipline keeps you steady. Flexibility keeps you alive. Without flexibility, even the most honourable commitment can slowly destroy you.

Chapter 2

Bhima Drinking Poison: Survival Matters More Than Prediction

Bhima was the strongest among the five brothers. He was physically powerful, fearless, and straightforward. Because of this, his cousins, the Kauravas, saw him as a serious threat.

From a young age, Duryodhana, the eldest of the Kauravas, felt insecure about Bhima. Bhima's strength, confidence, and popularity made it clear that if a conflict ever happened, defeating him openly would be very difficult. So Duryodhana chose a different path.

Instead of facing Bhima directly, he decided to remove him secretly. One day, during a meal, Duryodhana mixed poison into Bhima's food without anyone noticing. There was no warning.

No visible danger. No chance for Bhima to protect himself.

Bhima ate the food, completely unaware. The poison started working. His body weakened. He lost consciousness. Believing him to be dead, Duryodhana ordered that Bhima's unconscious body be thrown into a river.

This was not a fair fight. It was betrayal. A silent attempt to eliminate a problem before it could grow.

But Bhima did not die.

His physical strength, natural toughness, and powerful body helped him survive. Even after the poison entered his system and he was thrown into the river, he lived.

In time, Bhima returned. Not because he predicted the attack. Not because he avoided danger. But because he was strong enough to survive something he never saw coming.

That is the most important part of this story. Bhima did not win because he was smarter than Duryodhana. He survived because even when something went terribly wrong, he did not collapse permanently.

THE INVESTMENT TRUTH: Financial Shocks Rarely Announce Themselves

Most investors think danger will give signals in advance.

They expect problems to look like:

- bad news beforehand
- clear warnings
- expert predictions
- obvious signs

But real financial trouble rarely arrives that way.

It comes suddenly. A market crash. A sudden job loss. A medical emergency. A policy change. A company failure no one expected.

This is the "poison" in investing. It enters quietly. And by the time you realise what is happening, the damage has already begun.

The investors who survive are not the ones who predicted every crisis. They are the ones who were prepared to handle shocks. Just like Bhima.

THE LESSON: Build for Survival, Not Perfection

Bhima's story teaches a simple but powerful lesson.

You cannot predict every danger.
You cannot avoid every mistake.
You cannot control everything that happens.

> But you can decide whether a shock will destroy you or whether you will recover from it.

In investing, survival strength means things like:

- spreading your money instead of putting it all in one place
- keeping an emergency fund
- not borrowing excessively to invest
- not investing money you will need soon
- having realistic expectations
- having proper insurance

A fragile portfolio needs everything to go right. A strong portfolio can survive when things go wrong.

This is the 2nd lesson of Kurukshetra of Investing:

You don't need to predict every poison. You need the strength to survive it.

Markets will hit you unfairly at times. Your job is not to be perfect. Your job is to stay standing.

Chapter 3

Yudhishthira's Dice Game: Overconfidence Destroys Wealth

Yudhishthira was known as a good man. He was calm, thoughtful, respected, and trusted by everyone around him. More importantly, he believed strongly that he always acted with fairness and integrity. Over time, that belief slowly became his weakness.

After building a prosperous kingdom, Yudhishthira was invited by his rivals to a game of dice. It did not look dangerous. It was presented as a friendly game. A formality. Something connected to pride and honour.

Yudhishthira knew that dice games could be risky. He was not foolish. But deep inside, he believed something quietly and confidently:

"I am a fair man. I will not lose unfairly." That assumption changed everything.

Once the game began, Yudhishthira started losing. At first, the losses were small. Then they grew larger. Each time he thought, "One more round. I can recover." He did not stop. He did not step back. He did not question whether the situation itself was dangerous. He kept playing, not because it made sense, but because he believed he could not be completely defeated.

Eventually, he lost his wealth. Then his kingdom. Then his freedom. And finally, his dignity.

The tragedy was not the dice. The tragedy was believing that being a good person meant he could not lose. Yudhishthira did not lose because he was careless. He lost because he believed defeat was unlikely for him.

THE INVESTMENT TRUTH: Confidence Without Risk Control Is Dangerous

Many investors enter investments because something sounds convincing. They read a newspaper article saying a sector will do well. A friend talks confidently about a stock. Someone on social media explains why a commodity is the "next big thing." A book or video creates excitement.

So they invest. But they don't have a clear plan.

I once knew someone who invested a large part of his savings into a very popular new opportunity because everyone around him seemed confident about it. In the beginning, small gains made him feel he had made a smart decision. But when the trend reversed, losses started appearing. He had never decided how much risk he was willing to take or when he should step back.

Each fall only increased confusion. Should he holdṢ Invest moreṢ ExitṢ Because there was no plan, every option felt risky. So he did nothing and simply stayed invested, hoping things would somehow recover.

Most investors never ask themselves in advance:

- "If this goes wrong, what will I doṢ"
- "How much loss can I tolerateṢ"
- "When should I review or step backṢ"

They enter with hope, not clarity. When losses appear, confusion begins. They don't know whether to stay invested, invest more, or exit. So they continue simply because they don't know what else to do.

This is where many investors lose money. Not because the idea itself was terrible, but because there was no plan around the idea.

Long-term investing is not about holding anything forever. It is about entering with clarity and staying disciplined within that clarity. Just like Yudhishthira, the problem is not entering the game. The problem is entering without knowing where the game must stop.

THE LESSON: Knowing When to Stop Is a Skill

Yudhishthira's real mistake was not agreeing to play. It was not knowing when to stop.

In investing:

- Discipline means staying invested when your plan says so.
- Wisdom means recognising when your exposure has become too high.
- Patience means waiting for the right opportunities.
- Intelligence means setting limits before emotions take over.

Every strong investment plan has boundaries: how much risk to take, how your money is divided, when to rebalance, and when to exit. Without limits, even good intentions can become harmful.

Confidence is necessary to invest. But confidence without structure becomes overconfidence. And overconfidence is expensive.

This is the 3rd lesson of Kurukshetra of Investing:

Markets don't care how good you are. They only care how prepared you are.

Overconfidence destroys wealth quietly, politely, and completely.

Chapter 4

Shakuni's Psychology Trap: How Decisions Get Hijacked

Shakuni was not a great fighter. He didn't win battles with strength or weapons. Still, he became one of the main reasons for the destruction that followed. His real weapon was not power. It was understanding people's minds.

Shakuni knew one simple truth. If you control how a person feels, you can control what they do.

He never forced anyone. He didn't shout, threaten, or push

openly. Instead, he influenced people quietly. He stirred emotions. He planted thoughts. He created situations where others felt they were making their own decisions, while he was guiding everything from behind.

During the dice game, Shakuni didn't drag Yudhishthira to play. He didn't threaten him. Instead, he used very normal human weaknesses. Pride. The hope of winning back losses. Fear of looking weak. The need to prove oneself.

Every throw of the dice created tension. Every loss was followed by a simple line: "Just one more round." Slowly, clear thinking disappeared. Emotions took over.

Yudhishthira believed he was still in control. But in reality, his feelings were being pulled in a direction he didn't realise.

That is Shakuni's trap.

THE INVESTMENT TRUTH: Most Investors Don't Lose to Markets. They Lose to Influence.

Investors like to believe they are independent thinkers. But most financial decisions are shaped by external voices.

News headlines. Social media posts. Friends' success stories. "Expert" predictions. WhatsApp forwards. Market noise.

None of these force you to act. They simply create emotional pressure.

- Fear when markets fall.
- Excitement when markets rise.
- Anxiety when others make money.
- Urgency when "opportunities" are highlighted.
- Regret when you didn't act earlier.

Just like Shakuni, modern financial noise never says, "Make a bad decision."

Instead, it says:

- "Don't miss out."
- "Everyone is doing this."
- "This time is different."
- "You can recover quickly."

And when emotion rises, logic quietly leaves. The dangerous part is this: you feel like the decision was entirely yours.

HOW THE TRAP WORKS (WITHOUT YOU REALISING IT)

The psychological trap usually follows a predictable pattern.

First, discomfort is created. Something feels wrong. Markets fall. Others seem to be earning more. A new opportunity looks exciting.

Then urgency is added.

- "Act now."
- "Limited time."
- "Don't wait."

Then reassurance follows.

- "Low risk."
- "Safe bet."
- "Strong fundamentals."

By the time you act, you are no longer thinking calmly. You are reacting emotionally.

Just like Yudhishthira, the issue is not lack of intelligence. It is emotional manipulation.

THE LESSON: If You Don't Control Your Inputs, You Won't Control Your Outcomes

Shakuni's lesson is uncomfortable but essential. If you allow uncontrolled inputs, you will make uncontrolled decisions.

In investing, protection looks like:

- Limiting how much market news you consume
- Avoiding constant comparison with others
- Not reacting to daily price movements
- Having rules decided before emotions arise
- Trusting a long-term framework over short-term noise

Strong investors don't need more information. They need less emotional disturbance.

The goal is not to avoid influence completely. That's impossible. The goal is to prevent influence from making decisions for you.

This is the 4th lesson of Kurukshetra of Investing:

When someone else controls your emotions, they control your money.

When you feel urgency, pause.
When you feel excitement, slow down.
When you feel fear, step back.

That pause is where clarity lives.

Chapter 5

Draupadi's Humiliation: When You Don't Draw the Line Early

The most damaging moments in life rarely begin as sudden disasters. They usually start as small things that nobody stops in time. Draupadi's humiliation did not begin when she was dragged into the royal hall. It began much earlier.

It began when Yudhishthira agreed to sit at the dice table again. It continued when he kept playing after the first loss. It worsened when no one around him said, "Stop." And it became impossible to reverse when limits were crossed again and again without resistance. By the time Draupadi was brought into the hall, the real damage had already been done.

The tragedy was not just what happened to her. The tragedy was that **every step leading to it was allowed.** At every stage, someone could have intervened. Someone could have drawn a line. Someone could have said,

"This has gone too far." But no one did. Silence replaced action. Pride replaced restraint.

Discomfort replaced courage. And once the line was crossed publicly, the consequences kept growing. Anger. Humiliation. Loss of dignity. Years of suffering. And eventually, war. One boundary that was not protected early turned into a catastrophe later.

THE INVESTMENT TRUTH: Most Financial Damage Starts With a Small Boundary Violation

This is how most investors actually get into trouble. They don't lose money because of one sudden mistake. They lose money because small warning signs are ignored again and again.

It usually starts quietly.

- They take a little more risk than they planned. "Just this once."
- They delay fixing their portfolio. "I'll handle it later."
- They ignore discomfort. "It should improve."
- They postpone decisions. "Let me wait a little longer."
- They avoid facing reality. "Maybe things will turn around."

Nothing feels dangerous at first. Each step looks small. But each step weakens protection. Slowly, the original plan disappears.

By the time panic selling happens, the real mistake happened much earlier. By the time discipline breaks, rules had already been ignored many times. By the time serious losses appear, the warning signs had been visible for a long time.

Markets do not suddenly destroy investors. Investors slowly move away from their own safeguards. And once those safeguards are gone, emotions take control.

THE LESSON: Draw Your Financial Lines Before Emotion Forces You To

Draupadi's story is not only about humiliation. **It is about what happens when boundaries are not protected early.**

In investing, these boundaries include things like:

- how much risk you will take
- how much loss you can tolerate
- how your money is divided across investments
- clear reasons to invest and clear reasons to exit
- rules to follow during market ups and downs These are not restrictions. They are protection.

Strong investors do not rely on willpower when things become stressful. They rely on rules they decided when they were calm. Because once fear or hope takes over, clear thinking becomes very difficult.

This is the 5th lesson of Kurukshetra of Investing:

If you don't protect your financial limits early, your emotions will cross them for you later.

Chapter 6

The Pandavas Living Incognito: Progress Without Proof

After losing their kingdom and going through years of hardship, the Pandavas faced one final condition. They had to live for one full year hiding who they really were. No one should recognize them. If even one person identified them, everything they had endured would become useless and they would have to start over.

This created a strange situation. They had to live carefully and behave normally, but there was no way to know whether they were succeeding. No one would come and tell them that they were safe.

Arjuna, once known as a great warrior, worked as a dance teacher.

Bhima, famous for his strength, quietly worked in a kitchen. Yudhishthira, a natural king, served as a court assistant.

Most importantly, no one was there to reassure them that their act was working. No one said, "You are safe. No one can recognize you." There was no sign at all that they were doing well.

No milestones. No appreciation. No confirmation.

Only one rule: if they stayed disciplined for the full year, they would succeed. If they slipped even once and someone recognized them, they would fail immediately.

This is the hardest kind of discipline. Not when results are visible, but when you must keep going without any proof that it is working.

They did not know whether their efforts were paying off. They only knew that one mistake would undo everything. So they focused on doing the right thing every day, not on getting reassurance.

THE INVESTMENT TRUTH: Most Investors Quit Because They Don't See Proof

This is where investing becomes difficult for many people.

Not during crashes. Not during losses. But during long periods when everything feels slow and uneventful. Your SIP is running. Your portfolio is stable. Markets are calm. Returns look ordinary.

There is no clear sign saying, "You are doing the right thing." No excitement. No visible reward. Nothing to celebrate.

This is when people start disturbing good plans.

They begin to wonder:

- "Is this even workingṢ"
- "Should I change somethingṢ"
- "Others seem to be doing better."
- "Maybe I should try something new."

Nothing is actually wrong. But the silence itself becomes uncomfortable.

Just like the Pandavas, investors often have to continue without

immediate proof. And this is where real discipline is tested.

THE LESSON: Discipline Means Acting Correctly Even When Results Are Invisible

The Pandavas survived that year not because they were powerful, but because they followed one simple rule. Do the right thing every day, even when nobody confirms it.

In investing, this means:

- continuing SIPs even when returns look boring
- staying invested when markets feel dull
- not changing plans just to feel active
- trusting long-term strategy over short-term excitement

Most investors don't fail because they chose bad investments.

They fail because they cannot tolerate long periods without visible progress. They mistake calm periods for failure.

This is the 6th lesson of Kurukshetra of Investing:

Progress does not always show itself immediately. Discipline means continuing even without reassurance.

If your investments feel quiet, stable, and uneventful, it does not mean nothing is happening. It often means the process is working.

Chapter 7

Krishna Chooses Peace Over Army: Guidance Is More Powerful Than Tools

As the conflict became unavoidable, both sides approached Krishna for support. Everyone expected him to choose a side by offering military strength. He had powerful armies, influence, and resources. If he wanted, he could tilt the outcome of the war.

But Krishna did something unexpected.

Instead of offering weapons or soldiers, he tried to prevent the war altogether. He went to Duryodhana with a simple proposal. Avoid war. Prevent destruction. Resolve the conflict peacefully.

Krishna did not come with force. He came with reason. With perspective. With concern for long-term consequences.

He did not demand kingdoms or power. He asked for a small compromise that could prevent massive loss of life.

Duryodhana rejected the proposal. He believed strength would win. He believed numbers mattered more than wisdom. He believed power was more important than foresight.

Krishna accepted the refusal and stepped back.

This moment reveals something important. Krishna did not measure success by winning an argument. He measured it by choosing the path that could avoid unnecessary destruction, even if it looked weak in the short term.

Peace was not weakness. It was wisdom that went unused.

THE INVESTMENT TRUTH: Tools Don't Replace Judgement

Many investors believe better tools will protect them.

- More data.
- More charts.
- More strategies.
- More products.
- More apps.

But tools don't think. They don't understand your life. They don't weigh consequences. They only help you act faster.

Just like Krishna's peace offer, good guidance often looks simple and unimpressive. A calm suggestion to slow down. A reminder to stay aligned with your goals. A warning against unnecessary risk.

These don't feel powerful. They don't feel exciting. So people ignore them.

Why Guidance is Most Valuable Before Damage Occurs

Most people appreciate guidance only after losses.

- After a bad investment.
- After panic selling.
- After a costly mistake.

But guidance is most valuable before anything goes wrong.

Krishna's effort was preventive. He tried to avoid damage, not repair it later.

In investing, good guidance helps you:

- avoid taking too much risk
- stay calm during emotional periods
- reduce unnecessary buying and selling
- protect long-term compounding

Tools help you act. Guidance helps you avoid acting when action would be harmful.

THE LESSON: Wisdom Is Not Loud

Krishna's choice teaches a mature lesson. Real power does not always look dramatic. It often appears calm, patient, and understated.

In investing:

- tools help you execute
- products help you participate
- markets create opportunities

But guidance helps you choose wisely.

This is the 7th lesson of Kurukshetra of Investing:

Guidance may not look powerful, but it quietly prevents the damage that aggressive action can cause.

In the long run, avoiding unnecessary loss is more valuable than chasing risky gains.

Wisdom protects wealth. Tools only move it.

Chapter 8

Duryodhana Rejects Krishna's Peace Offer: Stubbornness Is Expensive

By the time Krishna approached Duryodhana with a peace proposal, the situation was already tense. Conflict had grown, anger had built up, and war seemed close. But destruction was still avoidable.

Krishna did not come asking for surrender. He did not demand humiliation or total defeat. He offered a compromise that could prevent war and save countless lives.

The proposal was simple. Fair. Practical.

But it required Duryodhana to step back slightly. And that was the real problem.

Duryodhana did not reject the proposal because it was unreasonable. He rejected it because accepting it would mean admitting that he had gone too far. In his mind, stepping back would make him look weak. It would reduce his authority. It would damage his image.

So he refused.

Not after carefully analysing the consequences. Not after weighing what was best for everyone.

He refused because his ego was already deeply invested in the

path he had chosen. At that point, appearing strong mattered more than doing what was right.

And that decision made war unavoidable.

The price of stubbornness was not paid immediately. It was paid slowly in loss, destruction, and regret.

THE INVESTMENT TRUTH: Investors Don't Stick to Bad Decisions. They Stick to Their Ego

Many investors behave exactly like Duryodhana.

They are not ignorant. They are not careless. They are emotionally attached to decisions they made in the past.

They say:

- "I've already invested so much, I can't change now."
- "If I exit, it means I was wrong."
- "Let it recover, I'll decide later."
- "I don't want to book a loss."

This is not patience. It is ego trying to protect itself.

The decision is no longer about what will produce the best outcome. It becomes about avoiding the feeling of being wrong.

Instead of asking, "What is the right decision nowṢ" the investor starts asking, "How can I avoid admitting my mistakeṢ"

That question is expensive.

Why Stubbornness Costs More Than Mistakes

Mistakes can be corrected. Stubbornness delays correction.

The longer you refuse to adapt:

- losses increase
- new opportunities pass by
- your flexibility reduces
- emotional pressure builds

By the time action is finally taken, much of the damage has already occurred.

Duryodhana did not lose because he had no options. He lost because he refused to reconsider.

In investing, refusing to review, rebalance, or exit a weak position does not protect your money. It only allows the problem to grow.

THE LESSON: Flexibility Saves Money. Ego Burns It.

Duryodhana's story is not about judging him. It is a warning about a very human tendency.

Strong investors are not those who never make mistakes. They are those who recognise mistakes early and correct them.

Changing your mind is not weakness. It is intelligence responding to new reality.

In investing:

- reviewing your portfolio shows responsibility
- rebalancing shows maturity
- exiting a bad position is not failure
- adapting is survival

This is the 8th lesson of Kurukshetra of Investing:

Stubbornness may feel strong in the moment, but it is one of the most expensive habits in wealth creation.

Markets do not punish honest mistakes severely. They punish the ego that refuses to change.

Chapter 9

Choosing Krishna Over the Narayani Sena: Why Direction Beats Power

As the war became unavoidable, Krishna offered both sides a choice. But there was an important detail in how the choice was given. Arjuna was asked first.

Krishna presented two options.

On one side, Krishna offered himself alone. He would not fight. He would not use weapons. He would only guide, advise, and help with decisions.

On the other side, he offered his entire **Narayani Sena:** thousands of trained soldiers, weapons, and immense military strength.

Arjuna did not take long to decide. He chose Krishna.

Not because Krishna would fight for him, but because Krishna would help him think clearly when the situation became confusing.

Duryodhana watched this and could not believe it. In his mind, Arjuna's decision looked foolish. Why reject a powerful army and choose one unarmed person insteadṢ To him, this was not wisdom. It was weakness.

When his turn came, the Narayani Sena was the only option left. He accepted it happily. He believed he had made the smarter choice. Numbers, strength, and scale would surely decide the war.

From the outside, Duryodhana's decision looked sensible. But it revealed a deeper blind spot.

History gave the final answer. The Pandavas, who chose Krishna's guidance, won the war.

THE INVESTMENT TRUTH: The Best Choice Often Looks Weak at First

Most investors behave like Duryodhana, not because they are foolish, but because they are practical in the wrong way.

They are often given a similar choice.

On one side:

- high-return products
- impressive past performance
- complex strategies
- fast results
- big numbers

On the other side:

- clarity
- process
- discipline
- long-term thinking
- steady guidance

The second option looks boring. Too simple. Not exciting enough. So many people ignore it.

They choose power over perspective.

Arjuna chose clarity before the battle began. Duryodhana chose scale and hoped it would be enough.

This is why many people think having a financial planner or advisor is unnecessary. They believe everything is already available online.

Data is free. Charts are everywhere. Returns can be tracked instantly.

Just like Duryodhana, they assume information alone is enough

Why This Matters Most During Volatility

When markets are rising, almost everything seems to work.

But when uncertainty appears:

- products don't calm fear
- returns don't tell you what to do next
- numbers don't reduce anxiety

This is when clarity becomes valuable.

Arjuna did not need more weapons. He needed guidance when emotions could cloud judgement.

Investors who rely only on products feel confident during good times. During bad times, they feel lost.

They start asking:

- "What should I do nowŞ"
- "Should I exitŞ"
- "Should I change my strategyŞ"

That is when they realise what they did not choose earlier.

THE LESSON: Choose Direction Before You Need It

Arjuna's decision looked foolish to others at that moment. But mature decisions often look unimpressive to people who only value visible strength.

He chose guidance before uncertainty arrived, not after panic began.

In investing, this is exactly the role of a financial planner.

A good planner is not there to give you the biggest product, the fastest return, or the most complicated strategy.

The real value lies in:

- helping you think clearly during confusion
- preventing emotional decisions
- keeping you aligned with long-term goals
- guiding you when fear and greed rise

You may not notice this value every day. But when volatility hits, that guidance becomes decisive.

In investing:

- products can be replaced
- strategies change
- markets evolve

But clear thinking remains valuable in every situation.

This is the 9th lesson of Kurukshetra of Investing:

Power helps you act. Clarity tells you where to go.

Choose clarity first. Everything else works better after that.

Chapter 10

Kunti Revealing the Truth Too Late: Delay Is the Most Expensive Decision

Kunti carried a secret for most of her life. Before her marriage, she had given birth to a child through a divine blessing. That child was Karna. Because of fear, social pressure, and uncertainty, she was forced to abandon him. At that time,

staying silent felt like the only way forward.

As years passed, that silence became easier to maintain.

Karna grew up elsewhere. He built his own identity. He formed deep loyalties. He chose his friends and his path in life. Kunti knew the truth the entire time, but she kept postponing the moment to reveal it. Not because she didn't care, but because every passing year made the conversation more difficult.

Finally, just before the great war began, she went to Karna and told him the truth. She revealed that he was her son.

But by then, it was too late.

Karna had already committed himself to Duryodhana. His loyalties were set. His values were shaped. His decisions had already been made. The truth did not lose its importance, but it lost its power to change anything.

The tragedy was not the secret itself. The tragedy was the delay. The right truth, revealed at the wrong time, could no longer alter the outcome.

THE INVESTMENT TRUTH: Most Financial Mistakes Are Not Wrong Decisions. They Are Late Decisions.

Many investors already know what they should do.

They know they should:

- start investing early
- review their portfolio regularly
- have adequate insurance
- plan for future goals

But they postpone action.

- "I'll start next year."
- "Let things settle first."
- "I'll do it once I earn more."
- "I'll review later."

Delay feels harmless. It doesn't feel like a mistake. Nothing bad happens immediately, so it seems safe to wait.

But delay quietly increases the cost. The longer you wait:

- you lose valuable compounding time
- risks remain uncovered
- imbalances grow larger
- corrections become harder

By the time action is finally taken, the effort required is much greater.

Just like Kunti's truth, the decision itself may still be correct.

But its ability to change the outcome has weakened.

THE LESSON: Timing Gives Decisions Their Power

Kunti's story teaches a difficult but important lesson. Some decisions do not become wrong over time. They simply become less useful.

In investing:

- starting late means you must invest much more later
- fixing problems late means accepting bigger consequences
- planning late means compromising your goals
- reviewing late means reacting under pressure

Early action gives you choices. Late action leaves you with limited options.

This is the 10th lesson of Kurukshetra of Investing:

A delayed decision is often more costly than a wrong one corrected early.

In wealth creation, speed does not mean rushing. It means not postponing what you already know must be done.

The most expensive decision is rarely a bad one. It is the one you kept delaying even after knowing it was necessary.

Chapter 11

Dhrishtadyumna's Birth for a Purpose: Every Investment Needs a Mission

Dhrishtadyumna's story is unusual from the very beginning. He was not born by chance. He was born with a clear purpose.

From the moment he came into the world, everyone knew why he existed. His life had a single mission that is to defeat Dronacharya. Whether we agree with the reason or not does not matter here. What matters is the clarity. There was no confusion about his role. No doubt about his direction. No uncertainty about what he was meant to do.

As he grew up, everything he learned supported that one goal. His training, his decisions, and his preparation were all aligned with that purpose. Nothing was random. Nothing was wasted. There were no distractions pulling him in different directions.

Dhrishtadyumna did not try to become everything. He became exactly what he was meant to be.

THE INVESTMENT TRUTH: Money Without a Purpose Gets Misused

Most people start investing without clear intention.

They invest because:

- someone recommended it
- they had extra money lying around
- markets were rising
- friends were investing
- they felt they "should start"

But if you ask them one simple question "Why does this investment existṢ" they often don't have a clear answer.

When money has no purpose:

- it gets withdrawn casually
- it gets switched frequently
- it gets compared unnecessarily
- it gets disturbed by emotions

Just like a person without direction gets distracted easily, money without a purpose gets misused.

But when you know:

- this money is for retirement
- this is for a child's education
- this is for safety

- this is for long-term growth

Your behaviour automatically changes. You become calmer.

You stop reacting to every market movement. You stop expecting every investment to perform the same way.

Purpose gives money discipline.

THE LESSON: Assign a Job to Every Rupee

Dhrishtadyumna's strength came from clarity of purpose. In investing, clarity works the same way.

Every investment should have:

- a specific goal
- a time frame
- a clear role
- an acceptable level of risk

Not every investment needs to give the highest returns. Some are meant to protect your money. Some are meant to grow steadily. Some are meant to be available when you need them.

Problems begin when one investment is expected to do everything.

This is the 11th lesson of Kurukshetra of Investing:

When the purpose is clear, decisions become easy. When there is no purpose, mistakes increase.

Money works best when it has a job. Every rupee should know why it exists.

Chapter 12

Barbarik's Boon and Burden: Behaviour Decides Returns, Not Timing

Barbarik was a powerful warrior connected to the Mahabharata through his lineage. He was the grandson of Bhima and the son of Ghatotkacha. Though young, he possessed extraordinary strength and a rare boon that no other warrior had.

He had the ability to fight on the side that was losing at any given moment. Whichever side was weaker, Barbarik would support it. At first, this sounded noble and unbeatable. He would always stand with the disadvantaged.

But this ability also made him dangerous.

If Barbarik entered the war, the battle would never end. Every time one side began to lose, he would switch. And the moment he switched, the balance of power would change again. The losing side would become strong, and the other side would start losing. Then he would switch again.

The war would turn into endless chaos. Not because of lack of strength, but because of constant shifting. Barbarik was not ineffective due to weakness. He was ineffective because he could never stay on one side long enough for the battle to reach a conclusion.

That is why Krishna stopped him from entering the battlefield. Not because Barbarik lacked skill, but because his pattern of action would prevent any meaningful outcome.

THE INVESTMENT TRUTH: Switching Hurts More Than Bad Timing

Many investors behave exactly like Barbarik, believing they are being smart and responsive.

They say:

- "This fund is not doing well, I'll switch."
- "This sector is falling, I should exit."
- "That investment is performing better, I'll move there."

On the surface, this sounds logical. Support what is losing.

Move to what is winning. Avoid weak performers.

But this behaviour creates a damaging cycle.

I once knew my uncle's friend who kept moving his money repeatedly. First he put most of his savings into bank fixed deposits because they felt safe. When interest rates fell, he became unhappy and surrendered the deposits early to buy an insurance plan that promised better returns. After a few years, he realised the returns were modest and the lock-in was long, so he stopped paying premiums and moved the remaining money into a "high return" investment someone recommended. When that did not perform as expected, he shifted again.

Years passed. He had always been investing. But very little wealth had actually grown.

The problem was not the products. It was the constant switching.

By the time investor switch, the difficult period is usually almost over.

Just when things are about to improve, they move out.

And when the new investment starts doing well, they enter late again.

So they experience the pain, but miss the recovery.

Returns are not lost because of one bad decision. They are lost because of repeated changes. Just like Barbarik, the investor keeps changing sides and never stays invested long enough for compounding to work.

Why Behaviour Dominates Outcomes

Markets move in cycles. Interest rates change. Different products look attractive at different times. This is normal.

What destroys wealth is not choosing the wrong investment once. It is reacting to every change.

Barbarik's problem was not lack of power. It was his inability to stay put.

Similarly, investors often do not fail because:

- they chose bad investments
- they entered at the wrong time They fail because:
- they switch repeatedly
- they chase recent performance
- they abandon discipline

The biggest enemy of compounding is interruption

THE LESSON: Control Behaviour First. Timing Becomes Secondary.

Barbarik's story delivers a sharp lesson. If behaviour is unstable, no strategy can produce consistent results.

In investing, good behaviour looks like:

- staying invested through cycles
- avoiding frequent switching
- giving investments time to work
- accepting temporary underperformance
- following a long-term plan Bad behaviour looks like:
- reacting to short-term results
- constantly changing strategies
- chasing whatever worked recently
- abandoning investments during discomfort

This is the 12th Lesson of Kurukshetra of Investing :

Returns are not decided by when you enter. They are decided by how you behave after entering.

Timing gets attention. Behaviour gets results.

Chapter 13

Arjuna's Blind Spot: Clarity Beats Emotion

Arjuna was known as the greatest warrior of his time. If there was one person everyone trusted on the battlefield, it was him. He had trained for years, won countless challenges, and his aim was legendary.

But on the day of the biggest battle of his life, something unexpected happened.

As he rode to the front, he asked his charioteer, Krishna, to stop so he could see who stood on the opposite side.

When he looked closely, he froze.

The people standing there were not strangers. They were his own relatives, teachers, and elders. People he had grown up with. People who had guided him, blessed him, and shared his life.

In that moment, his strength felt useless. His training felt meaningless. His confidence collapsed.

His hands trembled. His bow slipped. He said, "I can't fight them. My mind is confused. I don't know what to do."

This was not fear of war. It was emotional overload.

Arjuna was overwhelmed by memories, relationships, and attachment. His judgement became clouded. His clarity disappeared. He could not make a decision.

So Krishna stepped in.

Krishna did not fight the battle for him. He did not remove the problem. He simply gave Arjuna clarity when Arjuna could not find it himself. He reminded him of his purpose. He helped him see the bigger picture beyond the immediate emotions.

Once clarity returned, Arjuna picked up his bow again. Not with anger or confusion, but with calm focus and purpose.

Nothing outside had changed. Only his understanding had.

THE INVESTMENT TRUTH: When You Look at Your Money Emotionally, You Freeze Like Arjuna

Every investor has their own "Arjuna moment."

When markets fall or uncertainty rises, they do not see numbers alone. They see:

- their savings
- their hard work
- their future plans
- their family's security

And suddenly, the mind panics.

Just like Arjuna, investors freeze when emotions take control. They think:

- "I can't handle seeing this loss."
- "What if things get worseṢ"
- "Should I stop investingṢ"
- "Should I exit and protect what is leftṢ"

I once saw this happen to a relative who had been investing steadily for years. When markets corrected sharply, he stopped his SIP because the falling values made him anxious. Months later, when markets recovered, he realised he had missed buying at lower prices. The problem was not the investment. It was the emotional reaction to temporary loss.

This is not lack of knowledge. It is emotional overload.

Fear blurs judgement. Attachment clouds thinking. Worst-case scenarios feel real even when they are not. Investors often damage their wealth not during the fall itself, but during the decisions made in panic.

THE LESSON: A System Gives You Clarity When Emotion Takes Over

Arjuna needed Krishna not because he lacked skill, but because he lacked clarity in that moment.

Every investor needs something similar. Not necessarily a person, but a system that guides decisions when emotions become overwhelming.

That system could be:

- a proper asset allocation
- a long-term financial plan
- disciplined SIPs
- a trusted advisor
- clear rules for action
- defined risk limits

Emotion says, "Do something right now."

Clarity says, "Do what is correct, not what feels urgent."

Investors who react emotionally often regret it. Investors who follow a system remain steady even in difficult times.

This is the 13th Lesson of Kurukshetra of Investing:

When emotion takes over, clarity disappears. When clarity returns, confidence returns.

Just like Arjuna, your decision-making becomes powerful again when you see the bigger picture calmly.

Chapter 14

Krishna Shows the Vishwaroopam: Perspective Changes Decisions

At the start of the war, Arjuna faced a moment of complete confusion. He was not weak. He was not unprepared. He was not inexperienced.

Yet his mind was overwhelmed.

He saw only what was directly in front of him. People he loved. People he respected. People he did not want to fight. That narrow view paralysed him.

At that moment, Krishna did not give Arjuna battle strategies or clever arguments. He did something far more powerful. He expanded Arjuna's perspective.

Krishna revealed the **Vishwaroopam** : a vision that showed reality on a much larger scale. Past, present, and future together. Creation and destruction together. The flow of time beyond one single moment.

Arjuna suddenly saw what he could not see before. This was not just one battle. It was part of a larger purpose, a larger timeline, and a larger reality.

Nothing outside changed. The battlefield was the same. The people were the same.

Only Arjuna's perspective changed.

And once his perspective changed, his confusion disappeared and his decision became clear.

THE INVESTMENT TRUTH: Narrow Views Create Bad Financial Decisions

Most investors face the same issue. Not lack of knowledge, but lack of perspective.

They focus only on what is happening right now:

- today's market value
- current interest rates
- recent losses or low returns
- short-term news
- temporary underperformance

When the view becomes narrow, fear grows.

- A small fall feels like a disaster.
- A temporary loss feels permanent.
- A short slowdown feels like failure.

Just like Arjuna, investors freeze not because the situation is hopeless, but because they are looking at it too closely.

The way to regain clarity is to widen your view deliberately (zoom out and see the bigger picture).

Instead of reacting to short-term movements:

Look at how your money is meant to serve your long-term goals, not just current returns.

Review whether your financial plan still makes sense overall, not whether one investment is disappointing.

Remember that different assets behave differently at different times - what looks weak today may provide stability later.

Avoid checking values too frequently during uncertain periods. Focus on the purpose of the money: safety, income, growth, or liquidity.

For example:

- An FD may look "low return" during high-inflation periods, but it provides stability and certainty.
- Insurance may feel like an expense until the day protection becomes critical.
- Gold may stay quiet for years and suddenly become valuable during crises.
- Equity investments may fluctuate sharply but reward patience over long horizons.
- Real estate may move slowly but serve as long-term security.

When you step back, you realise the goal is not to make every investment look exciting at all times. The goal is to make your overall financial life stable and capable of handling the future.

When attention shifts from "What is happening todayṢ" to "Is my long-term foundation intactṢ", fear reduces and clarity returns.

Why Long-Term Perspective Changes Everything

When you step back and look at a longer period:

- volatility starts to look normal
- temporary problems appear manageable
- time begins to work in your favour
- emotions settle down

What feels overwhelming today often becomes insignificant in a wider timeline.

Short-term events tell one story. Long-term patterns tell another.

Krishna did not change the war.

He changed how Arjuna saw the war.

Similarly, situations in life, career, health, or finances do not become easier just because you panic. But your decisions become wiser when you see the larger picture instead of reacting to the moment.

THE LESSON: Change the Frame, Not the Plan

The Vishwaroopam teaches a powerful lesson.

When decisions feel difficult, the problem is often not the situation itself. It is the way you are looking at it.

In investing:

- zooming out reduces fear
- context reduces anxiety
- perspective restores clarity

You do not need perfect timing.
You need patience and the right time horizon.

This is the 14th lesson of Kurukshetra of Investing:

When perspective expands, decisions simplify.

Short-term noise feels loud only when you stand too close.

Step back. The picture changes.

Chapter 15

Krishna Steering Arjuna's Chariot: Focus on Behaviour, Let Your System Guide Direction

In the war, Arjuna had one clear job. He was the archer. His responsibility was to aim, stay focused, and act at the right moment.

Krishna had a completely different role.

- He did not fight.
- He did not chase enemies.
- He did not get distracted by the chaos.

He drove the chariot.

Krishna handled direction, timing, and positioning. He made sure Arjuna was always placed where his skill would matter most. He adjusted movement as the battlefield changed, without disturbing Arjuna's concentration.

Because direction was taken care of quietly in the background, Arjuna could focus entirely on execution.

He didn't have to worry about where to go next.

He didn't have to analyse everything happening around him. He simply did his job well.

Execution stayed sharp because direction stayed steady.

THE INVESTMENT TRUTH: Performance Improves When Roles Are Clear

Many investors struggle because they try to handle everything themselves at the same time.

They try to:

- watch markets constantly
- analyse news
- control emotions
- change strategy
- make decisions
- execute actions

All together.

This overload creates confusion.

When emotions rise, direction changes. When direction changes, behaviour breaks.

Performance suffers not because of lack of intelligence, but because there is no separation of roles.

Consider two investors during a volatile market phase.

The first investor checks prices throughout the day. Every news update feels urgent. One day he thinks he should sell. The next day he considers buying more. Fear and hope keep pulling him in different directions. Because there is no clear structure, every movement feels like a decision point. Stress increases.

Mistakes follow.

The second investor behaves very differently. He already has a system. His portfolio is broadly structured. For example, 70% in equity for growth, 20% in debt for stability, and 10% in commodities for balance. He reviews the portfolio only once in six months and rebalances if needed. During market volatility, he does not redesign everything. He simply follows the structure already decided.

Both investors face the same market.

But their experience is completely different.

One reacts continuously. The other executes calmly.

In investing, results improve when direction and execution are handled separately.

- Your long-term plan decides the path.
- Your behaviour simply follows that path.

In investing, results improve when direction and execution are handled separately.

One part of your system decides the long-term path.

Another part focuses on consistent behaviour.

Why Systems Matter Most During Uncertainty

Markets don't become dangerous because of price movements alone. They become dangerous because of emotional pressure.

- Volatility creates noise.
- Noise creates anxiety.
- Anxiety creates impulsive decisions.

A system exists to absorb that pressure.

- Asset allocation
- pre-decided rules
- clear goals
- rebalancing plans
- disciplined processes

These don't remove uncertainty. They prevent panic from controlling behaviour.

Just like Krishna adjusted the chariot quietly, a good financial system adjusts direction without disturbing discipline.

THE LESSON: Don't Re-Think Direction in the Middle of Action

The biggest mistake investors make is trying to rethink everything when stress is high.

- They question their plan.
- They abandon structure.
- They react instead of execute.

That is when damage happens. The chariot lesson is simple:

You don't have to control everything.

You only need to control your behaviour and trust your system for direction.

This is the 15th Lesson of Kurukshetra of Investing:

Focus on doing the right actions consistently. Let your system handle where those actions lead.

When behaviour stays disciplined and direction stays stable, results follow naturally.

Chapter 16

Jayadratha's Escape and Return: One Weak Link Can Break the Entire System

The Pandavas had formed a strong circular defensive formation to protect Abhimanyu. Every warrior had a specific role.

Everyone knew where to stand and what to do. The system worked only as long as each person stayed in position.

Jayadratha's job was not to defeat the Pandavas. He didn't need to fight them head-on. His task was simply to block them for a short time. That alone was enough.

At a crucial moment, Jayadratha found a small opening in the formation. He positioned himself there and prevented the Pandavas from going back inside. For a brief period, support could not reach Abhimanyu.

That short delay changed everything. Abhimanyu was left alone inside the formation. No one could help him. A powerful system collapsed because of one small weak point. Jayadratha did not destroy the formation with strength. He broke it by blocking one critical connection.

THE INVESTMENT TRUTH: Strong Plans Fail at Their Weakest Point

Most financial plans look strong from the outside.

Investments are selected carefully.

Returns look reasonable. Goals are clearly defined.

Yet many plans fail. Not because everything went wrong, but because one small weakness was ignored.

I once knew a friend who had built a solid long-term investment plan. His portfolio was well diversified and meant for future goals. Everything looked stable.

But he kept almost no emergency fund, assuming his regular income would always support the plan.

Then an unexpected situation occurred. His income stopped temporarily for a few months. During that period, he needed money for daily expenses and commitments. Since there was no backup support, he was forced to withdraw from long-term investments at the worst possible time.

The investments themselves were not the problem. The plan failed because support was blocked when it was needed most. Just like Abhimanyu was left alone when help could not reach him, his financial plan collapsed because the backup system was missing.

Common weak spots that create such situations include:

- no emergency fund
- too much loan burden
- insufficient insurance
- irregular savings habits
- no liquid money for urgent needs

At the beginning, these don't look dangerous. But under pressure, they cut off support to the main plan. And once support stops, even a strong system can fail.

WHY SYSTEMS BREAK FROM THE EDGES

Big systems rarely collapse all at once. They fail when one weak area is exposed.

Jayadratha did not defeat the Pandavas. He only blocked support for a short time.

In the same way, financial plans don't collapse just because markets move. They collapse when life creates pressure.

- When income stops temporarily.
- When medical expenses appear suddenly.
- When urgent cash is needed.
- When discipline breaks.

At that moment, the missing piece becomes critical.

THE LESSON: Strengthen the Weakest Link First

Jayadratha's story gives a simple but important lesson. You don't need a perfect plan. You need a complete one.

Before trying to maximise returns, make sure the basics are strong:

- Keep an emergency fund
- Have proper insurance
- Control debt levels
- Maintain accessible savings
- Ensure steady cash flow

This is the 16th lesson of Kurukshetra of Investing:

A system doesn't fail where it is strong. It fails where it is ignored.

Good investing is not about making things complicated.

It is about removing the weak spots that can break everything.

Chapter 17

Abhimanyu in the Chakra~Vyuh: Every Entry Needs an Exit Plan

Abhimanyu was young, talented, and extremely brave. He knew how to break into the Chakra-Vyuh, a complicated circular battle formation designed to trap enemies. He had learned this from his father, Arjuna, who once explained it while Abhimanyu was still in his mother Subhadra's womb.

But there was one problem.

He learned how to enter the formation. He never learned how to come out.

When the time came, Abhimanyu entered the Chakra-Vyuh perfectly. His attack was bold and confident. At first, everything seemed under control. But once he moved deeper inside, the formation closed behind him. The path he used to enter disappeared. No one could reach him. There was no way out.

Abhimanyu fought with incredible courage. But courage alone could not replace a missing plan. The tragedy was not that he lacked skill. The tragedy was that his preparation was incomplete.

THE INVESTMENT TRUTH: Entering Is Easy. Exiting Is Where Most Investors Fail

Most investors spend a lot of time deciding what to invest in.

- They compare returns.
- They look at past performance.
- They listen to tips.
- They ask friends.

But very few think seriously about one important question:

How and when will I take the money outȘ

For example, someone may invest aggressively for a child's education, but when the admission year arrives, the market may be down and the money is still exposed to risk. Another person may invest for buying a house but never plan when to shift the funds to safer options. When the time comes, they are forced to sell at whatever value is available.

Entering an investment feels exciting. Exiting feels uncomfortable. So exits are delayed again and again, or decided suddenly when emotions are high.

Why Goals Require Ęxit Planning

Every investment is meant for something.

A child's education. Retirement. A house. Financial security.

But if there is no plan for withdrawing the money at the right time, the goal becomes risky.

Many investors don't think about:

- when they will actually need the money
- how to reduce risk as that time approaches
- how to protect what they have built
- what to do if markets fall at the wrong time

Goals usually don't fail because markets move.

They fail because the exit was never planned.

THE LESSON: Decide the Exit Before You Enter

The story of Abhimanyu gives a simple but powerful lesson.

Before investing, decide:

- What is this money forṢ
- How long can it stay investedṢ
- When should risk be reducedṢ
- Under what situation should I review this investmentṢ

Once you are inside the market, emotions become stronger and decisions become harder. Planning exits in advance removes panic later.

This is the 17th lesson of Kurukshetra of Investing:

An entry without an exit plan is not confidence. It is vulnerability.

Strong investors don't predict perfectly. They align investments to goals and prepare completely.

Chapter 18

Karna and the Kavacha-Kundala: When Principles Turn Into Risk

Karna lived by one strict personal rule. Anyone who came to him asking for help would never be refused. He followed this rule throughout his life without exception.

At the same time, Karna was born with a natural protection called the Kavacha-Kundala, an armour that made him almost

impossible to defeat. He did not earn it. It was always with him, silently protecting him.

One day, Indra came to Karna in the form of a Brahmin and asked for his Kavacha-Kundala as charity. Karna immediately understood what was being asked. Giving away the Kavacha-Kundala would remove his protection. He knew it would make him vulnerable in battle. But refusing would break the rule he had followed all his life.

So Karna did what he always did. He chose consistency over safety. Without hesitation, he gave away the very thing that protected him.

Karna did not lose because he lacked values. He lost because he followed his principle blindly, even when the situation had changed. A rule that once made him admirable quietly became the reason for his downfall.

THE INVESTMENT TRUTH: Discipline Without Context Is Dangerous

Most investors admire discipline. And rightly so.

They create strong personal rules:

- "I will never sell."
- "Long-term means I won't change anything."
- "I will always stay fully invested."

- "Keeping cash is a waste."
- "I will invest only in fixed deposits."
- "I won't surrender this insurance policy even if the returns are low."

These rules are not wrong. In fact, they often work for many years.

The problem begins when life changes but the rules don't.

- Income may change.
- Responsibilities may increase.
- Goals may get closer.
- Risk tolerance may reduce.

But the investor continues following the same rule mechanically.

At that point, discipline stops protecting wealth and starts exposing it.

Why Systems Fail At The Worst Moment

Karna didn't need to abandon his principle entirely. He needed a boundary. One exception.

One condition. One adjustment. But rigid systems don't allow judgment.

In investing, this rigidity shows up when:

- portfolios are not de-risked near goals
- asset allocation is not reviewed after life events

- liquidity is ignored because "long-term means long-term"
- rules are followed even when assumptions break

One of my uncle's friends strongly believed that "insurance is a waste if I don't get money back." Because of this belief, he refused to buy pure protection plans and did not take health insurance either. He kept only traditional policies that offered some savings or maturity value, because that had been his rule for many years.For many years, nothing seemed wrong.

Premiums were paid. Policies continued. He felt secure.

Then a major medical emergency struck the family. The insurance coverage turned out to be far too small. He had to break fixed deposits, borrow money, and sell investments at the worst possible time.

The problem was not lack of discipline. He had been consistent for years. The problem was that his rule never evolved. Protection had quietly become insufficient, but he never reviewed it.

But the investor continues following the same rule mechanically.

At that point, discipline stops protecting wealth and starts putting it at risk.

THE LESSON: Principles Must Protect You, Not Test You

The story of the Kavacha-Kundala teaches a simple but powerful lesson. Principles are meant to support outcomes, not override common sense.

In investing:

- discipline is important
- systems are useful
- consistency matters

But none of these should be applied blindly. They must adjust when risk changes. They must adapt when life changes. Their purpose is protection, not stubbornness.

This is the 18th lesson of Kurukshetra of Investing:

The most dangerous rule is the one you refuse to adjust.

Wealth is not destroyed by lack of discipline. It is destroyed when discipline is applied without judgment.

Chapter 19

Ghatotkacha and Timing: Use Strength Only When It Is Required

Ghatotkacha was one of the most powerful warriors in the war. He was especially dangerous at night. In darkness, his strength would multiply, making him almost impossible to stop.He could grow in size, move unpredictably, create terrifying illusions, and attack from directions no one could anticipate.

Soldiers could not even tell where the attack was coming from.

Krishna knew how devastating this power was. Yet Ghatotkacha was not used early in the war.

This was not hesitation. It was strategy.

Karna possessed a divine weapon called the Vasavi Shakti, given by Indra. This weapon could kill any opponent with certainty, but it could be used only once.

Karna had saved this weapon for one person alone: Arjuna.

As long as Karna still possessed it, Arjuna's life was in constant danger.

If Ghatotkacha had been sent into battle earlier, Karna would not have been forced to use this weapon. Ghatotkacha was dangerous, but not Karna's main target. Karna could have fought him using conventional weapons and preserved the Vasavi Shakti for Arjuna.

Krishna understood this clearly. So he waited. Time passed. The war intensified.

Bhishma had fallen. Dronacharya was now leading, but the pressure was mounting. The Kaurava army was bleeding resources. Then came the night battle, a period of extreme and unpredictable volatility where Ghatotkacha unleashed chaos. It was at this stage, even before he took full command, that Karna had to step in as the main pillar to prevent a total market collapse.

At that stage, Karna was no longer just another warrior. He had become the main pillar holding the army together.

Then came the night battle.

Ghatotkacha attacked with overwhelming force. In darkness, his powers multiplied. He created confusion through illusions, destroyed battle formations, and spread panic everywhere.

Ordinary soldiers could not stop him. Even powerful warriors struggled to counter him.

The army began to break apart. Now Karna faced a crisis.

There was no Bhishma to stabilise the situation. No Drona to neutralise the threat. No strong backup remaining. If Ghatotkacha was not stopped immediately, the Kaurava army could have suffered catastrophic losses that very night.

Karna had no safe option left.

He could either preserve the Vasavi Shakti for Arjuna and risk losing the army, or use it now and sacrifice his greatest advantage forever.

Under extreme pressure, he chose to save the army.

Karna released the Vasavi Shakti. The divine weapon struck Ghatotkacha and killed him instantly.

But in that same moment, Karna lost the one weapon that could certainly defeat Arjuna.

Ghatotkacha was not sent to win the war. He was sent to force Karna into using his ultimate weapon at the wrong time.

His sacrifice permanently shifted the balance of the war.

THE INVESTMENT TRUTH: Strong Resources Lose Value If Used Too Early

Many people weaken themselves financially without even noticing it. Not because they are careless, but because they use their strongest resources for everyday comfort.

For example:

- Using emergency savings for vacations or gadgets
- Breaking long-term investments just to upgrade lifestyle
- Taking loans even when income is steady
- Using retirement money for short-term needs

I know someone who had a solid emergency fund built over years in his Liquid Mutual Fund. But he used a large portion of it for a house renovation because things were going well. It didn't feel risky at the time. Later, when an unexpected job disruption happened, he realised the protection he had built was no longer there.

Nothing terrible happens immediately. Life continues normally. So it feels harmless.

But when a real crisis arrives like job loss, illness, major expense the protection is already gone.

Just like using Ghatotkacha too early would have wasted him, using your financial safety nets casually removes your protection when you truly need it.

Why Holding Back Is Actually Wise

Krishna did not delay because he was confused. He delayed because he was clear.

He knew:

- Not every problem needs your strongest solution.
- If you use your power early, you become weak later.
- Patience keeps options open.

In real life, this looks like:

- Keeping emergency funds untouched for true emergencies
- Allowing long-term investments to grow without interrupting them
- Solving small problems with small solutions
- Saving big actions for big situations

Strength is not about reacting fast.

Strength is about knowing when not to react.

THE LESSON: Preserve Strength Until the Situation Demands It

Ghatotkacha's story gives a very practical lesson.

Your resources are not meant to make life easy every day. They are meant to protect you when life becomes difficult.

In personal finance:

- Emergency money is for emergencies, not convenience
- Financial buffers are for shocks, not impatience
- Long-term investments are for goals, not impulses

This is the 19th lesson of Kurukshetra of Investing:

If you use your strongest resource early, you won't have it when it truly matters.

Wealth grows not by constant action, but by disciplined restraint and decisive use.

Chapter 20

Krishna's Strategy Against Drona: "Ashwathama Is Dead"

Half-Truths Don't Mislead You. They Disable You.

Dronacharya was not defeated by strength. He was defeated when his certainty broke.

As long as Drona believed his son Ashwathama was alive, he fought without hesitation. His mind was steady. His judgement was clear. No one on the battlefield could overpower him.

Krishna understood this. Drona could not be defeated through direct combat. He could only be weakened by breaking what he believed to be true.

So a plan was made.

An elephant named Ashwathama was killed. Then Yudhishthira, who was known for always speaking the truth, said loudly, "Ashwathama is dead."

This statement was technically true. But it was incomplete.

Yudhishthira then added softly, "It was an elephant, not his son." At that exact moment, Krishna blew his conch shell loudly. The powerful sound drowned out the final words so Drona could not hear them.

Drona heard only the first part. Ashwathama is dead.

Because the words came from Yudhishthira, he believed them immediately. He assumed his son had been killed.

In that instant, grief shattered his focus. His confidence collapsed. His mind became clouded. He stopped fighting. He laid down his weapons.

And in that moment of broken certainty, he was killed.

Drona did not fall because of a lie. He fell because he acted on an incomplete truth.

THE INVESTMENT TRUTH: Half~Truths Usually Come From Outside You

Most investors are not destroyed by bad intentions. They are influenced by external narratives.

What they hear often comes from:

- media headlines
- friends and relatives
- social conversations
- success stories of others

Many of these statements are not completely wrong. But they are only partially true.

They are not connected to:

- your income stability
- your financial goals
- your investment time horizon
- your risk tolerance
- your emotional comfort with volatility

And that gap is where mistakes happen. Just like Drona.

I know a retired professional who received a large lump sum after retirement. His entire future income depended on how that money was used. A relative suggested buying a villa in a gated community nearby, saying the rental income there was very high and consistent.

The suggestion sounded convincing. The relative himself was earning good rent from a similar property.

But there was one crucial difference.

The relative already had other income sources and did not depend on that rent alone for survival. He also had a tenant who happened to be a close acquaintance.

The retired person had no such backup.

After buying the villa, the property remained vacant for almost two years. No tenant came forward. During that time, there was no rental income, but maintenance expenses

continued. Since his entire retirement plan depended on that income, the situation became stressful very quickly.

The advice was not wrong. Rental yield in that area was indeed high. But it was not suitable for his personal situation.

That is exactly how half-truths cause damage.

The statement he heard was technically correct. But it was incomplete for his reality.

Why Media And Friends Create Dangerous Confidence

Media speaks in averages. Friends speak from their personal experiences. Neither speaks from the full details of your life.

A fund recommendation. A strategy that worked for someone else. A confident opinion repeated many times. All of this begins to sound convincing.

Not because it is entirely correct. But because it is incomplete.

When information is not filtered through your personal context, it creates confidence without protection.

And confidence without alignment is dangerous.

THE LESSON: Truth Is Only Useful When It Is Personal

The real lesson from the "Ashwathama is dead" moment is simple.

Information must be complete and relevant to your situation before you act on it.

In investing:

- general truths must be connected to personal reality
- strategies must match your risk capacity
- ideas must align with your timelines
- confidence must come from suitability, not popularity

This is the 20th lesson of Kurukshetra of Investing:

A half-truth does not confuse you. It gives you confidence without safety.

Wealth is not destroyed because investors don't know anything. It is destroyed because they act on information that was never meant for their situation. If the truth is not personalised, don't act on it.

Chapter 21

The Fall of Shalya: How Negative Voices Kill Good Decisions

Shalya was a highly skilled and experienced warrior. He was respected and capable. But during the war, he was not fighting on his own. He became Karna's charioteer. His job was simple. Guide the chariot. Support Karna. Boost his confidence.

But Shalya did the opposite.

Instead of encouraging Karna, he kept discouraging him. He pointed out Karna's weaknesses again and again. He compared him with Arjuna. He questioned whether Karna could really win. He kept planting doubt at the worst possible moments.

Karna did not suddenly lose his strength or skill. But his confidence slowly weakened. Doubt entered his mind. Hesitation replaced clarity. His decisions became slower and less certain.

Karna did not lose because he lacked ability. He lost because the person beside him kept pulling him down mentally. The wrong influence was sitting in the most important place.

THE INVESTMENT TRUTH: Decisions Die Quietly Under Negative Influence

Most investors don't fail because they chose the wrong investment. They fail because of the constant negative opinions around them.

Not open criticism. Not obvious bad advice. Just small, repeated doubts from people around them.

Comments like:

- "This won't work."
- "You should have sold earlier."
- "Why are you still holding thisṢ"
- "Others are earning better elsewhere."

These statements don't sound harmful. They sound like concern. They sound practical. But hearing them repeatedly slowly destroys confidence.

Just like Shalya never attacked Karna directly, negative voices don't touch your money. They weaken your thinking.

Why Wrong People Are More Dangerous Than Wrong Markets

Markets go up and down openly. You can see it. You expect it. But people influence quietly.

A bad market tests your patience. A negative environment destroys it.

Shalya did not reduce Karna's strength. He made him uncertain.

In real life, this happens when:

- You change your plan because others keep questioning it
- You switch investments mid-way due to outside opinions
- You lose confidence even though nothing has fundamentally changed
- You start doubting every decision you make

Eventually, you stop trusting your own plan. That is when even good decisions collapse.

THE LESSON: Protect Your Decision Environment

Shalya's story teaches one uncomfortable truth. Skill alone is not enough. You also need the right support.

In investing, confusion usually doesn't come from lack of information. It comes from too many opinions.

- You don't need to listen to every suggestion.
- You don't need to act on every concern.
- You don't need constant feedback from everyone around you.

What you need is the right guidance, not more noise.

I remember a new client who approached us for investment planning. After understanding his goals, we gave him a detailed proposal and recommended starting a disciplined SIP.

He went back, discussed it with friends, and later returned saying:

"My friend told me you are suggesting regular mutual fund plans. He said there is a direct option where I can invest on my own and save costs. So I'll handle it myself."

There is nothing wrong with choosing direct plans if someone understands what they are doing and has the discipline to manage it consistently.

But in this case, the decision was not based on clarity. It was based on someone else's opinion.

Three years later, he came back again. This time his tone was different.

He said:

"I actually started SIP for a few months, but then I stopped. Budget issues came up. Markets were also not doing well at that time. Now I feel if I had just continued for those three years, I would have accumulated a good amount because markets recovered strongly after the fall."

The issue was not regular vs direct.

The issue was lack of support and discipline.

- Without guidance, temporary problems became reasons to stop.

- Without conviction, market volatility felt threatening.
- Without accountability, consistency broke.

A decision influenced by someone else ended in hesitation and quitting.

This is the 21st lesson of Kurukshetra of Investing:

A good plan surrounded by negativity will fail. A strong strategy weakened by doubt will collapse.

Choose carefully who influences your financial decisions.

Because markets don't usually destroy good plans. People around you often do.

Chapter 22

Karna's Wheel Stuck in the Mud: Liquidity Saves You When Everything Else Collapses

Karna was fully ready for the battle. He had great skill. Years of experience. Powerful weapons. Strong confidence.

Nothing was missing.

But at the most important moment, something simple went wrong. His chariot wheel got stuck in the mud. He could not move forward. He could not turn. He could not defend properly.

Karna asked his charioteer, Shalya, to help lift the wheel. But Shalya refused and distanced himself, leaving Karna to struggle alone.

Now Karna was alone.

The battlefield did not defeat Karna. His situation did.

He tried desperately to pull the wheel out by himself. He struggled. Time passed. In that short moment when he was stuck and vulnerable, Arjuna attacked and killed him.

Karna did not lose because he lacked strength.

He lost because he lost mobility and support at the exact moment he needed it most.

THE INVESTMENT TRUTH: Illiquidity Turns Strength Into Weakness

Many people look financially strong on Paper.

They have:

- valuable property
- large investments

- long-term savings
- good income

On paper, everything looks impressive.

But when an emergency happens, they struggle. Not because they are poor, but because their money is locked.

They have wealth, but not usable cash.

They have assets, but not access.

Just like Karna's chariot, everything seems fine until movement is required.

A famous actress was once at the peak of success (I am not mentioning her name out of respect). She earned enormous wealth, owned properties, and was known for her generosity. She helped many people financially during her successful years. Friends, relatives, staff, and people in need all benefited from her kindness.

But later in life, when she faced serious financial and health difficulties, much of her wealth was tied up in assets that could not easily be converted into cash. Income had reduced, expenses had increased, and immediate funds were limited.

What made the situation even harder was that many of the people she had helped earlier were not able to support her when she needed help the most.

Her problem was not lack of success. It was lack of liquidity and dependable support during uncertainty.

This is a painful but practical reality. Past generosity, fame, or property cannot replace accessible money when life becomes difficult.

Why This Problem Shows Up Only During Crisis

During normal times, liquidity feels unnecessary.

- Cash feels like it is "not earning."
- Emergency funds feel excessive.
- Flexible savings feel boring compared to investments.

So people put almost everything into long-term plans, property, or locked products.

Nothing goes wrong for years. Then suddenly life happens.

- A medical emergency
- Job loss
- Business slowdown
- Unexpected major expense

Now money is needed immediately. But it cannot be accessed quickly without loss or delay. And that delay creates panic.

My professor once shared a story about his own family.

After their father passed away, he and his brother received an inheritance. Both invested the money, but in different ways.

His brother put almost everything into land and long-term bonds. On paper, his wealth looked very high. But most of it was locked and could not be converted to cash quickly.

My professor, on the other hand, also invested in land and bonds but kept a portion in flexible forms like fixed deposits, mutual funds, and gold.

A few years later, their mother suddenly fell seriously ill and required immediate hospital treatment.

His brother struggled to arrange money. Selling land would take time. Breaking bonds meant loss and delay. His wealth existed, but he could not use it when it mattered.

My professor simply pledged his gold and arranged cash quickly. Treatment began without panic.

Both brothers were equally wealthy. Only one was financially prepared.

That is the real power of having liquid assets along with longterm investments.

THE LESSON: Always Preserve the Ability to Move

Karna's story teaches a very practical lesson. You don't need flexible money every day.

But on the day you need it, nothing else can replace it.

In real life:

- Cash is not useless. It is safety.
- Liquid savings are not inefficiency. They are freedom.
- During a crisis, access matters more than total wealth.

People who survive financial shocks are not always the richest. They are the ones who can access money quickly.

Karna still had everything. Skill. Power. Weapons. Experience.

Confidence.

But long before that moment, he had already lost key protections and benefits.

His divine armour had been given away.

His one-time ultimate weapon had already been used.

His support system was weak. Even his charioteer refused to help him.

So when the crisis came, he had no backup left. In that final moment, he had no real options.

Not because he was weak, but because all his safeguards had

been exhausted earlier.

In life too, People don't usually fall because of one sudden problem.

They fall because when the problem comes, they have nothing left to rely on.

This is the 22nd lesson of Kurukshetra of Investing:

Liquidity may not increase your returns. But it can save you when everything else goes wrong.

When life gets difficult, survival is not decided by how much you own.

It is decided by how easily you can use it.

Chapter 23

Bheema's Vow to Break Duryodhana's Thigh: The Power of Focused Execution

Bhima was not known for clever tricks or complicated strategies. He was known for one thing, clear intent and dependable action.

After Draupadi was humiliated, Bhima made a vow. He declared that one day he would break Duryodhana's thigh in battle.

At that moment, it sounded emotional and intense. But what mattered was not the emotion. It was the clarity of his goal.

Years passed after that promise. During those years, many things changed. Alliances shifted. War plans became more complex. Strategies evolved.

But one thing did not change. Bhima did not forget what he had committed to do.

He did not talk about it constantly.

He did not try to act too early. He did not get distracted.

He simply kept the goal in mind, trained quietly, and stayed prepared.

When the final battle arrived, it did not require brilliance. It required execution. Duryodhana was skilled, strong, and confident.

But in the decisive moment, Bhima did exactly what he had prepared for over many years. No hesitation. No overthinking. No last-minute change of plan.

He did not try to be clever. He simply executed what he had committed to do.

And that was enough.

THE INVESTMENT TRUTH: Most Investors Fail at Execution, Not at Ideas

Most investors actually know what they should do.

They know they should:

- stay invested
- continue SIPs
- rebalance periodically
- avoid panic decisions
- think long term

The problem is not lack of knowledge. The problem is execution when it really matters.

Many investors begin with a clear goal. For example, saving for a child's education in 15 years or buying a home after a decade.

But as time passes, distractions appear. Markets move up and down. New opportunities look attractive. Short-term wants feel urgent. Fear and excitement keep changing.

Some investors lose focus.

- They use the money for something else.
- They postpone contributions.
- They change direction midway.
- They forget why they started.

When the real moment arrives, they are not prepared.

Wealth is rarely built by doing something brilliant at exactly the right time. It is built by doing simple things consistently and executing them when the purpose finally arrives.

That is where most people fail.

THE LESSON: Prepare Quietly, Execute Decisively

Bhima did not win because he was smarter than everyone else. He won because he never lost sight of the goal. He waited patiently, prepared steadily, and when the moment came, he acted without hesitation.

In investing, consistency means:

- staying committed to the original goal
- not getting distracted by market noise
- continuing SIPs even during downturns
- using the money only for the purpose it was meant for

Brilliance often gets distracted. Consistency remembers the goal.

This is the 23rd lesson of Kurukshetra of Investing:

You don't need to be brilliant all the time. You need to stay focused on the goal and act when the moment truly arrives.

That is how long-term wealth is actually built.

Chapter 24

Ashwatthama's Rage: Revenge Decisions Burn Your Future

Ashwatthama was the son of Dronacharya. His whole life revolved around his father. Drona was not just a teacher to him. He was his pride, support, and emotional anchor.

During the war, Dronacharya was killed through a clever plan, not in a straightforward fight. Ashwatthama did not see his

father fall in battle like a warrior. He saw him lose hope, put down his weapons, and die. That moment broke him completely.

The war did not stop his pain. The Kauravas lost. Duryodhana fell. The fighting was basically over. But Ashwatthama's anger was not over. He did not calm down. He did not think clearly. He wanted revenge.

One night, he secretly entered the Pandava camp, believing the Pandavas were sleeping there. In his mind, he was finishing the war. But he never checked properly. The Pandavas were not there.

Blinded by anger, he attacked and killed the sleeping sons of the Pandavas, thinking they were the Pandavas. Only later did he realise the truth. He had not destroyed the Pandavas. He had killed their children. He had destroyed their future, not their present.

This act did not bring his father back. It did not change the result of the war. It only crossed a line that could never be undone.

When the Pandavas found out, they hunted him down. Cornered and terrified, Ashwatthama made another terrible decision. In panic, he released the Brahmastra, a powerful divine weapon, to destroy the Pandavas.

Krishna immediately warned him not to use it. But Ashwatthama then realised something frightening. He knew how to release the weapon, but he did not know how to stop it.

Unable to control what he had started, he redirected the weapon toward Uttara, the pregnant wife of Abhimanyu, trying to kill the unborn child. This was no longer revenge. It was blind destruction.

Krishna again intervened and protected the child.

Ashwatthama, however, did not escape punishment. Krishna cursed him to live forever without peace, wandering the earth in pain, loneliness, and regret. The war had ended, but his suffering had only begun. His future was destroyed by the decisions he made after everything was already over.

THE INVESTMENT TRUTH: The Most Damaging Decisions Are Made After the Loss

Most investors do not destroy their wealth during a market fall. They destroy it after the fall, when emotions take over.

After losses, people feel angry. Angry at markets. Angry at investments. Angry at advice. Angry at themselves.

And anger wants action.

So people start doing things just to stop the pain:

- They sell everything to "end the stress."
- They give up long-term plans out of frustration.

- They take risky bets hoping to recover quickly.
- They lose trust in all investing systems.

But these actions don't recover losses. They make the damage permanent.

In the war, Ashwatthama's worst act did not happen during the battle. It happened after the war had already ended.

In the same way, investors often hurt themselves most after the crisis is over.

Why Revenge Decisions Feel Powerful

When you feel helpless, doing something feels better than doing nothing.

Ashwatthama did not act because it would help him. He acted because he could not bear the pain inside him.

Investors behave the same way.

They don't sell because it is the best decision.

They sell because holding feels painful.

They don't change plans because it is wiser. They change because they want emotional relief.

That relief feels good for a short time. But the financial damage can last for years

The Lesson: Protect the Future When You Are in Pain

Pain passes. Markets recover. Time heals both losses and emotions.

But decisions made in anger can destroy long-term wealth permanently.

Ashwatthama's story shows this clearly. His life was not destroyed by the war itself, but by what he did afterward.

In investing, the same rule applies:

- When emotions are high, pause.
- Avoid irreversible decisions.
- Give yourself time to calm down.
- Protect your future even if the present feels unbearable.

Markets move on. The real question is whether your decisions will allow your wealth to move on too.

This is the 24th Lesson of Kurukshetra of Investing:

The decisions you make after a loss determine your future more than the loss itself.

Most damage does not happen when things go wrong. It happens when pain pushes you to act without clarity.

Chapter 25

Krishna Breaking His Vow: Wisdom Is Choosing What Works, Not What Looks Right

Before the Kurukshetra War started, Krishna made a clear promise in front of everyone. He said he would not fight in the war, would not use any weapon, and would only serve as Arjuna's charioteer. And he kept that promise. He drove the

chariot, guided Arjuna, and stayed out of direct combat.

Meanwhile, Bhishma was almost impossible to stop. He was defeating Pandava soldiers one after another. Arjuna had the skill to fight him, but he held back. Bhishma was not just an enemy. He was someone Arjuna loved and respected deeply, almost like a grandfather. Because of that emotional conflict, Arjuna could not fight with full strength.

Krishna saw this clearly. He realized that if Arjuna continued to hesitate, the Pandavas would lose, not because they were weaker, but because Arjuna could not act decisively.

Krishna urged him to fight. Still, Arjuna hesitated.

So Krishna did something shocking. He suddenly stopped the chariot, jumped down, picked up a broken chariot wheel from the ground, and started walking toward Bhishma as if he was going to attack him.

Everyone was stunned. Krishna had promised not to fight, yet here he was, stepping into battle with a weapon in his hand.

But Krishna did not actually intend to kill Bhishma. His goal was to wake Arjuna up from his hesitation. Bhishma himself understood this. Instead of resisting, he lowered his weapons in respect, ready to accept whatever Krishna chose to do.

That moment shook Arjuna. He realized he had been holding back when the situation demanded action. His confusion cleared. He regained his focus, picked up his bow properly, and started fighting with determination again. Seeing this, Krishna returned to the chariot.

Yes, technically Krishna had broken his promise. But he did it for a bigger purpose. The promise mattered, but saving the right outcome mattered more.

THE INVESTMENT TRUTH: Rules Are Meant to Protect You, Not Trap You

Many people follow strict financial rules.

- "I will never sell."
- "I will never change my investment plan."
- "I will always stay fully invested."
- "I will never keep cash idle."

These rules sound disciplined and responsible. And often they work for a long time.

But life and markets change. Situations change. A rule that once protected you can start hurting you if you follow it blindly.

Why Krishna's Action Matters

Krishna did not ignore principles. He used judgment.

He understood that:

- rules / vows are meant to serve a purpose
- promises should not destroy the outcome
- rigid thinking can be dangerous

If Krishna had strictly followed his promise and done nothing, the Pandavas could have lost because Arjuna was too hesitant to fight Bhishma with full force at that time.

Sometimes doing what looks "correct" is not the same as doing what is truly right.

THE LESSON: Wisdom Is Context, Not Compliance

Discipline is important. Systems are important. Rules are useful.

But they are not permanent laws. In real life:

- adjust plans when life changes
- reduce risk when responsibilities grow
- protect money when conditions worsen
- adapt calmly instead of reacting emotionally

This is the 25th Lesson of Kurukshetra of Investing:

Doing the right thing is not always about following rules perfectly.

It is about understanding what the situation truly needs.

Rules guide you.

Judgment protects you.

And long-term success comes from using both together.

Conclusion

Kurukshetra Never Really Ended

Kurukshetra was not just one war in history. It is something that

Keeps repeating in different forms. Every generation faces its own version of it, not with weapons but with pressure, uncertainty, and difficult choices. In investing, this inner battle appears as fear versus discipline, impatience versus long-term growth, noise versus clarity, and ego versus good judgment. The names may change, but human behaviour does not. Arjuna's hesitation still appears when emotions rise. Bhishma's rigidity shows up when people refuse to adapt. Karna's misplaced loyalty appears in stubborn decisions. Drona's fall to incomplete information happens when people act on half-understood advice. Ashwatthama's rage appears when decisions are made in anger after losses. And Krishna represents calm guidance when everything feels confusing.

The true lesson of Kurukshetra is not about victory. It is about how decisions are made under pressure. Most wealth is not destroyed because people lack knowledge.

It is destroyed because actions are taken at the wrong time, for the wrong reasons, under the wrong influence. Markets will rise and fall. Uncertainty will return again and again. That part cannot be controlled. What matters is how you respond. Investors who succeed are not always the smartest or most aggressive. They are the ones who keep some money easily available instead of chasing every return, use judgment instead of blindly following rules, stay patient when nothing needs to be done, act firmly when action is truly required, refuse to let fear, pride, or anger control their decisions, and seek guidance that helps them think clearly. Krishna never promises certainty. He offers clarity, and clarity is enough.

If this book has served its purpose, it has not given you predictions or shortcuts. It has given you a way to think. A way to question advice, ignore unnecessary noise, recognise emotional traps, and pause before making rushed decisions. Your own Kurukshetra will appear again and again, during market falls, tempting opportunities, painful losses, and moments of doubt. When that happens, remember that the real battle is not outside. It is inside your decisions, and the choices you make repeatedly will shape your future.

A Note on GSM Investment Services

This book is not written to sell products or promise outcomes. It is written to address the behavioural side of money, the part that quietly determines success or failure long before returns appear. GSM Investment Services was founded by Mr.Ganesan Muralidharan and, with 24 years of experience, continues as a second-generation financial planning practice now led by his son, Vishal Muralidharan (the author), built on longterm thinking, discipline, and clarity. The aim has always been simple: to help individuals and families make sensible financial decisions, remain steady during uncertain times, and avoid costly mistakes driven by emotion. The focus is not on chasing the next opportunity but on building structure, patience, and alignment with real-life goals. This book reflects the same philosophy. Markets will change, products will evolve, and strategies will come and go, but behaviour will continue to decide outcomes. GSM Investment Services works with investors who value clarity over noise, discipline over excitement, and long-term thinking over short-term reaction. If this book resonated with you and you feel comfortable connecting with us, you may reach out at gsminvestmentservices.01@gmail.com

www.ingramcontent.com/pod-product-compliance
Lightning Source LLC
LaVergne TN
LVHW100321210926
848480LV00003B/1214